TRACE LETTERS AND NUMBERS

Children's Reading & Writing Education Books

BABY PROFESSOR

EDUCATION KIDS

Practice writing letters and numbers

A is for Airplane

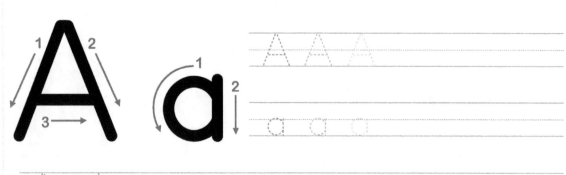

B is for Butterfly

B   b

B B B

b b b

Butterfly

C is for **Cake**

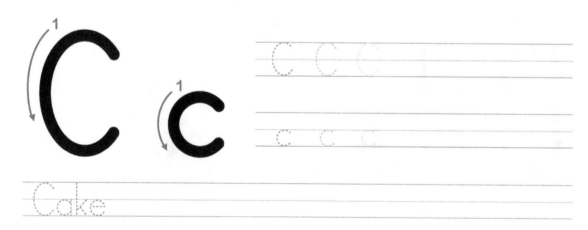

D is for Donut

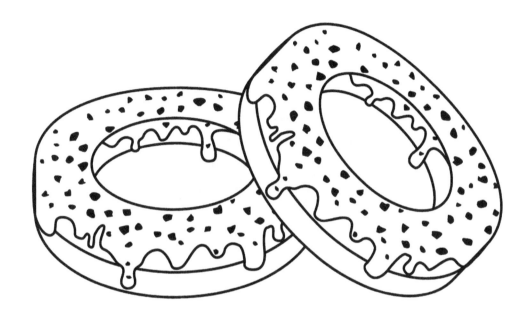

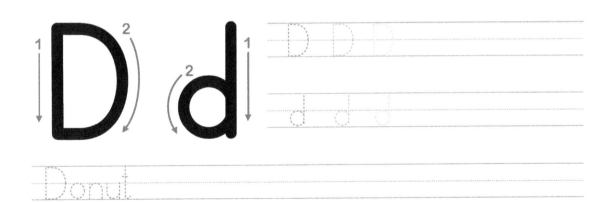

E is for **Eagle**

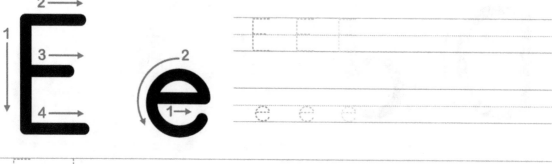

F is for Fish

G is for Gumball

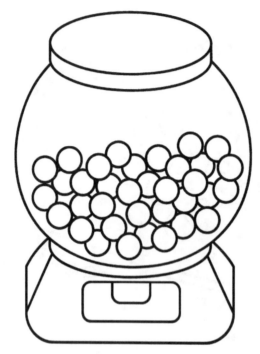

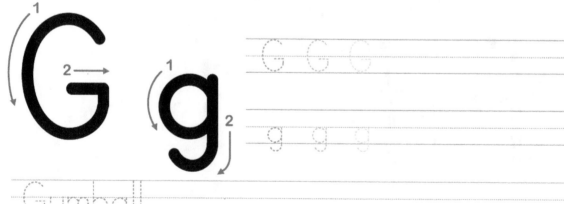

H is for **House**

I is for **Ice Cream**

Ice Cream

J is for **Jam**

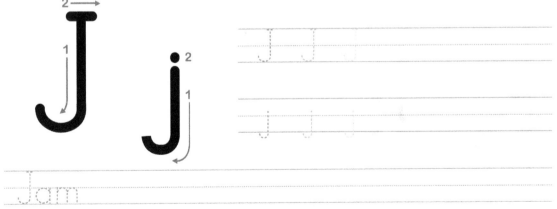

K is for **Koala**

K k

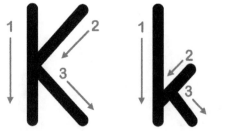

L is for **Ladybug**

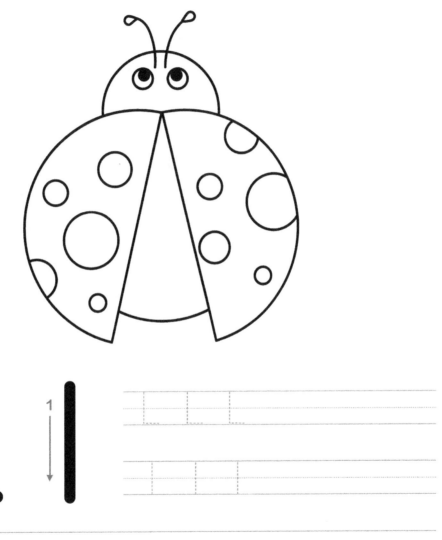

1↓ **L** 2→   1↓ **l**

Ladybug

M is for Monkey

M m

M M M

m m m

Monkey

N is for **Nest**

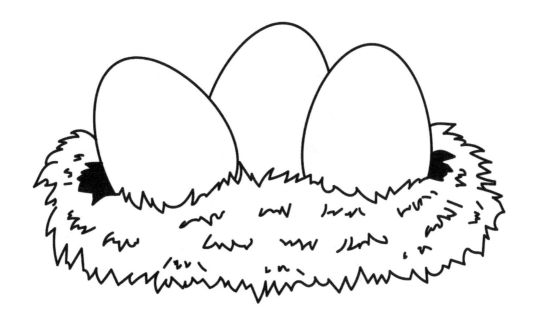

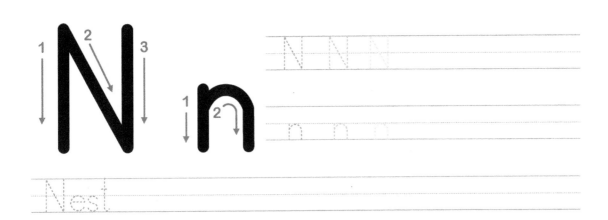

O is for Owl

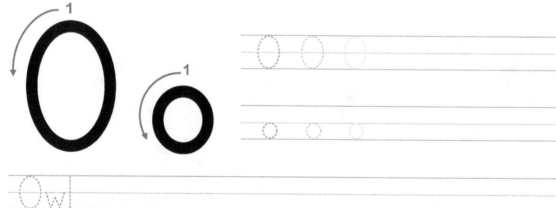

P is for **Penguin**

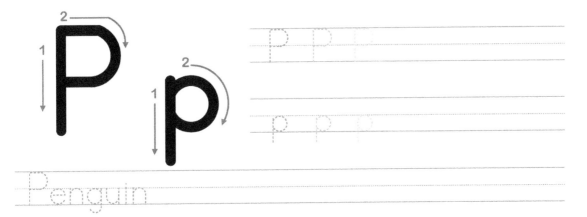

Q is for Queen

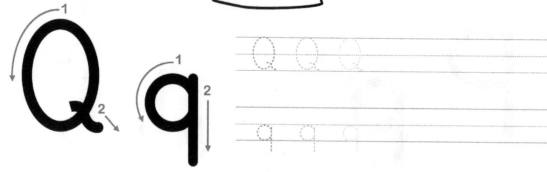

Queen

R is for Rainbow

R

r

R R R

Rainbow

S is for Sun

S s

S S S

S S S

Sun

T is for **Tree**

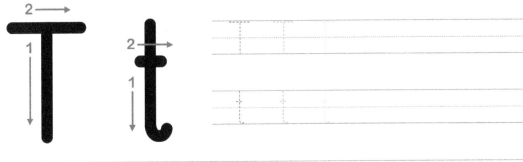

U is for **Umbrella**

Umbrella

V is for Vegetable

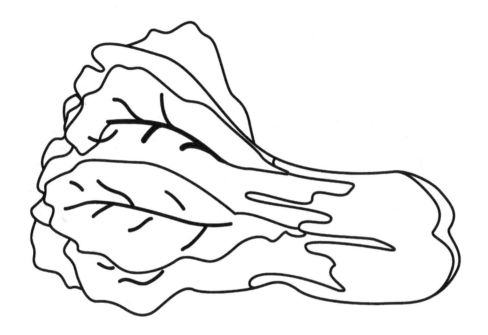

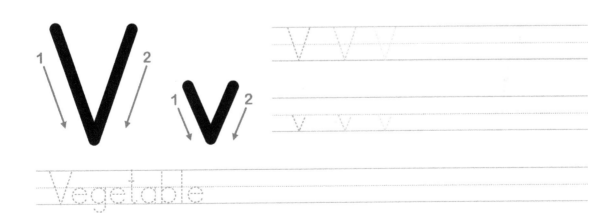

Vegetable

W is for Watermelon

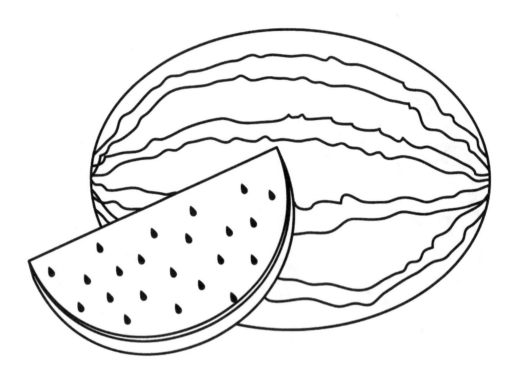

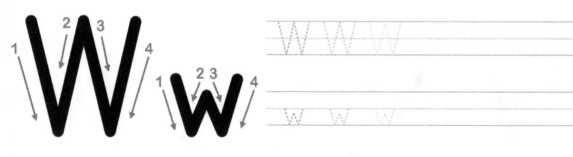

X is for Xylophone

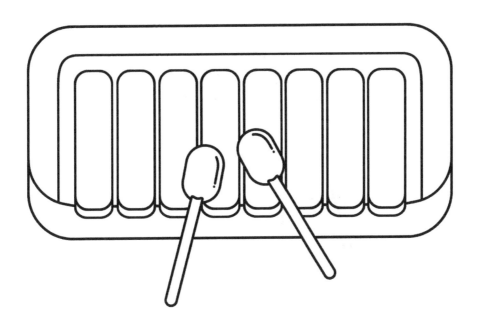

X X X

X X X

Xylophone

Y is for Yacht

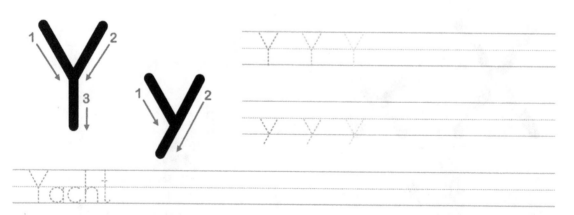

Z is for Zip

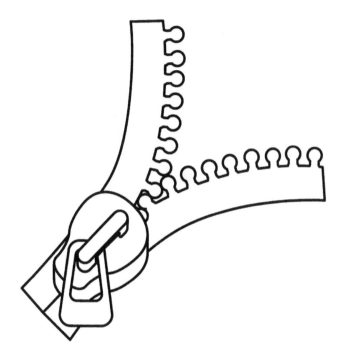

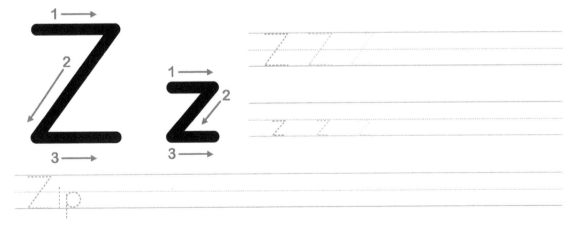

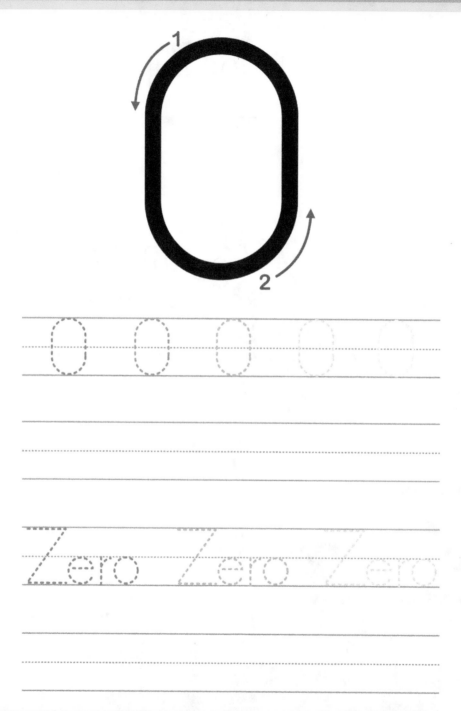

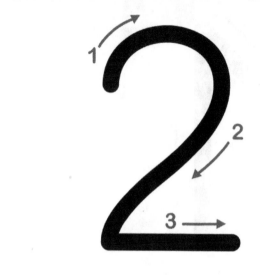

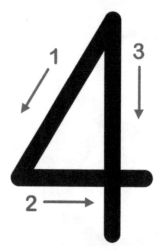

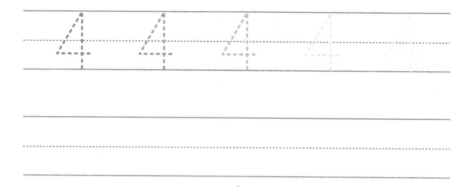

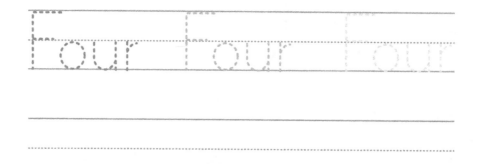

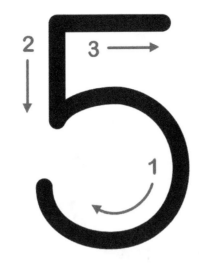

5 5 5 5 5

Five Five Five

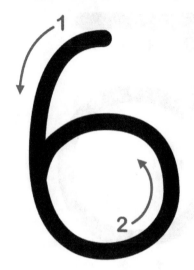

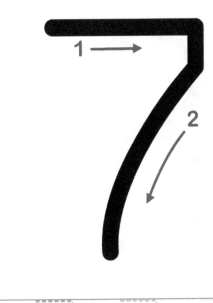

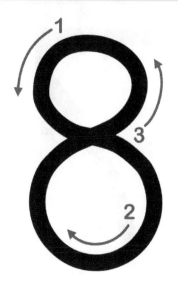

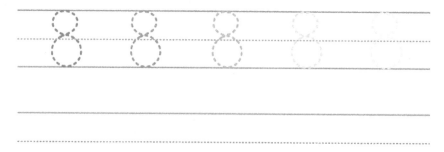

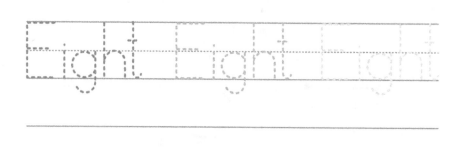

CPSIA information can be obtained
at www.ICGtesting.com
Printed in the USA
BVHW061332140321
602500BV00029BA/347

9 781683 264095